Our Changing World

THE TIMELINE LIBRARY

THE HISTORY OF THE TELEPHONE

BY BARBARA A. SOMERVILL

| 1850 | 1900 | 1950 | 2000 | 2050 |

Content Adviser: Ed McDonald, Museum Exhibit Director, Museum of Science and Industry, Chicago, Illinois

THE CHILD'S WORLD® • CHANHASSEN, MINNESOTA

Published in the United States of America by The Child's World®
PO Box 326 • Chanhassen, MN 55317-0326 • 800-599-READ • www.childsworld.com

ACKNOWLEDGMENTS
The Child's World®: Mary Berendes, Publishing Director

Editorial Directions, Inc.: E. Russell Primm, Editorial Director; Katie Marsico, Associate Editor and Line Editor; Judith Shiffer, Assistant Editor; Matt Messbarger, Editorial Assistant; Susan Hindman, Copy Editor; Sarah E. De Capua, Proofreader; Peter Garnham, Olivia Nellums, Molly Symmonds, and Stephen Carl Wender, Fact Checkers; Tim Griffin/IndexServ, Indexer; Cian Loughlin O'Day, Photo Researcher; Linda S. Koutris, Photo Selector

The Design Lab: Kathleen Petelinsek, Design and Art Production

PHOTOS
Cover/frontispiece images: Bettmann/Corbis (main); Photodisc/Punchstock (left inset); E. Russell Primm (right inset).

Interior: Bettmann/Corbis: 7, 10, 13, 23, 25; Corbis: 20 (Underwood & Underwood), 29 (Peter Beck); Getty Images: 5 (Taxi/Stephen Simpson), 26 (Newsmakers/Sean Gallup); The Granger Collection: 8, 14, 19.

Timeline: Bettmann/Corbis: 18, 25; Corbis: 12 (Schenectady Museum; Hall of Electrical History Foundation), 28 (Reuters); Getty Images/Photodisc/Ryan McVay: 22; Library of Congress: 6, 9, 11, 15, 21; Pictures Now: 10, 17 (Thomas Eakins), 20, 27 (David Lissy).

LIBRARY OF CONGRESS CATALOGING-IN-PUBLICATION DATA
Somervill, Barbara A.
   The history of the telephone / by Barbara A. Somervill.
      p. cm. — (The timeline library (series))
   ISBN 1-59296-346-3 (library bound)
   1. Telephone—History—Juvenile literature. I. Title. II. Series.
   TK6165.S66 2004
   621.385—dc22   2004003737

TABLE OF CONTENTS

INTRODUCTION

A WORLD WITHOUT PHONES

4

CHAPTER ONE

THE NEED TO COMMUNICATE

6

CHAPTER TWO

EARLY ATTEMPTS AT A TELEPHONE

11

CHAPTER THREE

TALKING OVER A WIRE

14

CHAPTER FOUR

PLENTY OF CHANGES

21

CHAPTER FIVE

THE TELEPHONE TODAY

27

GLOSSARY

30

FOR FURTHER INFORMATION

31

INDEX

32

A WORLD WITHOUT PHONES

It's Monday morning. Everyone is in a rush. Dad quickly checks his e-mail. The doctor's office calls to remind Mom of her 9 o'clock appointment. Lilly gets a text message on her pager: "School pictures today . . . Anna." Sam's cell chimes—soccer practice is called off.

People in the United States make about 2 billion telephone calls each business day. Businesses order and sell products and services. Friends talk to friends. Parents call children. E-mail messages fly through space. Students do homework on the Internet. Sorrow, joy, anger, hope, and surprise speed along telephone wires.

Just suppose telephones did not exist. Life would slow to a snail's pace. Businesses could sell only to people who walked in the door or ordered by mail. Friends could not call friends. Information could not come instantly from mysterious cyberspace—there would be no cyberspace. How different our world would be.

Each day, millions of telephone calls travel across lines such as the ones shown here.

CHAPTER ONE

THE NEED TO COMMUNICATE

Drums pound in the jungles of Africa. The rhythm and notes send a message from tribe to tribe. Strangers are coming from the river.

On the Great Plains of North America, smoke rises in distinct puffs. A scout has found a bison herd to the southwest. The Lakota head out for the hunt.

In a backyard, two children stretch a length of string between two soup cans. "Can you hear me?" one whispers into the can. "Loud and clear," comes the answer.

For centuries, humans have needed to communicate over distances. Drums and smoke signals serve that purpose. So do flags, flares, bonfires, lanterns, carrier pigeons, and, yes, soup cans. Yet, those methods have limits.

1500s

Plains Indians communicate across long distances using smoke signals.

The Spanish explore Mexico and today's southwestern United States.

Drum signals work only if the receiver is in hearing range and understands the drumbeats. Distance restricts the success of smoke signals or ship flags. Even carrier pigeons could be downed by storms or birds of prey.

1607–1775: MAIL SERVICE

During the colonial days (1607–1775) in America, people communicated over distance by letter. Mail traveled between the colonies and Europe by ship. Weeks and even months could go by between the time a letter was sent and received. Or it might never be received. Sometimes, ships sank.

1600s

Mail travels by ship between the Jamestown colony and England.

Galileo puts together a long-distance telescope to observe the stars.

Plains Indians sent messages over long distances using smoke signals.

Stage coaches carried people and letters from one colonial city to another.

Within the colonies, riders or stagecoaches carried the mail. In 1673, New York governor Francis Lovelace began a postal service between New York and Boston. The service ran once a month—and this was considered an improvement!

Postal service improved after 1737. At that time, young Ben Franklin took charge of Philadelphia's postal service. Franklin planned new postal routes and faster methods of moving mail. His changes reduced mail delivery times, but letters were still slow to arrive.

1800s: HARNESSING ELECTRICITY

Throughout history, people watched horses run and wondered if they could move faster—perhaps with the help of a machine. Some people saw birds fly and wondered if they could fly, too. Not surprisingly, people did not dream about long chats with their friends on the telephone. Long-distance communicating had no "sample" to spur on invention. Before this could be imagined, several discoveries had to occur.

These discoveries dealt with electricity. Specifically, people did not know how to produce it, control it, or use it. During the early 1800s, several scientists studied electricity. In 1830, American scientist Joseph Henry

1729 — Stephen Gray sends electricity along a wire.

The first mathematics textbook ever to be published in the colonies is published in Boston.

1830 — Joseph Henry (left) sends an electric signal over a wire.

Peter Cooper builds America's first steam locomotive, the Tom Thumb.

Morse's telegraph made sending messages faster.

sent an actual signal along an electric wire. This was success!

Two years later, Samuel F. B. Morse began experimenting with sending entire messages by electricity. Early attempts to do so failed. In 1838, he introduced an alphabet made from dots and dashes—the Morse code. It took six more years before an message traveled by wire. In 1844, Morse sent the message, "What hath God wrought!" from Washington, D.C., to Baltimore, Maryland.

Finally, there was inspiration for the telephone. If dots and dashes traveled over a wire, a human voice could, too. The race was on to invent the telephone!

1838

Samuel F. B. Morse introduces the Morse code.

Cherokee people are forced to walk the "Trail of Tears" from Georgia to Oklahoma.

1844

Morse sends the first telegraph message.

The first private bathroom in a hotel is offered at the New York Hotel.

CHAPTER TWO

EARLY ATTEMPTS AT A TELEPHONE

Once the telegraph proved successful, inventors experimented with sending other sounds over electric wires. Four scientists gained fame for their efforts toward building a telephone. They were Philipp Reis, James McDonough, Elisha Gray, and Alexander Graham Bell.

In the early 1860s, Philipp Reis of Friedrichsdorf, Germany, invented the Reis **Transmitter** and the Reis **Receiver.** Many scientists believe that Reis's transmitter was the first machine to send a human voice.

Reis's transmitter design was simple. It had a metal contact against a paperlike **diaphragm.** A person spoke into a cone-shaped mouthpiece. The sound moved the diaphragm and forced contact with the metal. The Reis Transmitter was tricky. The diaphragm did not always work. Reis's receiver

1860	Philipp Reis develops the Reis Transmitter and the Reis Receiver.

Abraham Lincoln (right) is elected U.S. president.

used the strange scientific theory of **magnetostriction.** This theory stated that metals stretched or shrank when affected by a magnet. Reis's receiver worked—but not very well.

James W. McDonough of Chicago, Illinois, also experimented with the telephone. In fact, some people credit McDonough with the first working telephone. In 1875, he created the "teleloge," his version of a telephone. He applied for a **patent** on April 10, 1876.

The Patent Office rejected McDonough's application—eight years later. By that time, Alexander Graham Bell's telephone was already in thousands of homes and businesses.

James McDonough creates a device that transmits human voices.

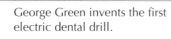

1875

George Green invents the first electric dental drill.

Elihu Thomson (left) operates the world's first radio.

McDonough appealed the Patent Office decision. One court declared McDonough's teleloge to have been developed before Bell's telephone. The Bell Telephone Company appealed that decision. A different court said Bell's invention was the first. Such confusion! Finally, Benjamin Butterworth, of the U.S. Patent Office, settled the argument in Bell's favor.

The U.S. Patent Office is located in Washington, D.C.

Alexander Graham Bell began experimenting with sound to help deaf people hear.

TALKING OVER A WIRE

Alexander Graham Bell never set out to invent the telephone. His main goal was to improve life for the deaf. This was a natural interest. Both Bell's mother and his wife were deaf.

As a child, Bell's parents encouraged learning, science, music, and curiosity. Two childhood events paved Bell's path to invention.

One came from an experiment with his mother. This experiment triggered his first thoughts about sending sound. He placed his lips on Eliza Bell's forehead and spoke against her skull. The bone passed on the **vibrations** of

1871 — Alexander Graham Bell begins teaching at a school for the deaf in Boston.

Orville Wright is born. He and his brother, Wilbur, will later go on to invent the airplane.

sound. Sound, he discovered, traveled like waves on water.

Then, Melville Bell suggested that his sons, Melly and Alexander, build a speaking machine. The young brothers created a model with a movable tongue, mouth, throat, nose, and lungs. The model could say "ma-ma," much to the surprise of visitors in the Bell home.

In 1871, Alexander Bell began teaching at a school for the deaf in Boston. There, he met Mabel Hubbard, to whom he became engaged in 1875. (They married in 1877.) Even with a teaching career, Bell hoped to continue experiments with electricity. He wanted to invent a multiple telegraph that would send several sounds at one time.

Bell met his wife, Mabel, at a school for the deaf in Boston, Massachusetts.

1875

Bell and Thomas Watson attempt to invent a multiple telegraph in the laboratory.

The Civil Rights Act is passed by Congress (left), giving African-Americans full access to public buildings.

Thomas Watson was Bell's laboratory assistant.

1875: A BREAKTHROUGH

With money from Mabel's father, Bell set up a laboratory. He hired Thomas Watson to help him. Bell designed a machine that would send sound from one place to another. He arranged musical reeds made of steel along a magnet. The reeds shook in response to a human voice. He hoped the magnet would react and send the sound. He called this invention a harp **apparatus.**

On June 2, 1875, the two inventors had a breakthrough. Bell was working in one room. Watson was in another. They were working with the harp apparatus. Watson's machine had one reed that stuck. When he released the stuck reed, it made a twanging sound. Bell

1875

Bell produces a harp apparatus that sends sound using reeds.

U.S. Congress passes a law introducing a 20-cent coin.

heard the sound repeated on his own machine.

Spurred on by this event, Bell designed several different reed-and-magnet machines. On February 14, 1876, he filed his plans for his invention with the U.S. Patent Office.

On March 10, 1876, Bell and Watson succeeded in sending a voice message from a transmitter to a receiver. Legend claims that Bell spilled acid on himself. To get Watson's help, he spoke into the transmitter, saying, "Mr. Watson, come here! I want you." Historians question the truth about the acid spill. They agree, however, that those were Bell's first words over a telephone. And Watson definitely heard the message.

> **FOCUS ON THE FIRST TELEPHONE**
> BELL RECEIVED PATENT NUMBER 174,465 ON MARCH 7, 1876, FOR IMPROVEMENTS TO TELEGRAPHY—BELL'S TELEPHONE. HISTORIANS BELIEVE THAT THIS PATENT MAY HAVE BEEN THE MOST VALUABLE PATENT EVER ISSUED.

Bell applies for a patent for his telephone.

The first major baseball league is founded with eight teams.

Bell and Watson continued to improve the design. Finally, they built a transmitter and receiver that worked reliably. It was time to show the public Bell's telephone.

1876: GRAY OR BELL?

Elisha Gray almost made it into the history books as the telephone's inventor. He drew a design of a workable telephone. Gray filed a **caveat** for a patent on February 14, 1876. Bell filed his own caveat on the same day but a few hours before Gray.

Gray, like McDonough, sued Bell and lost. Everything worked in Bell's favor. Normally, an inventor had to make a model from the design filed with the patent office. Bell received the patent without ever producing a

1876

Hires root beer (right) is
sold at soda fountains.

Mark Twain publishes *The
Adventures of Tom Sawyer.*

model. Later, scientists proved that Gray's design would have worked. They also showed that Bell's "patent model" would not. By then, it was too late for Gray.

Bell gained his patent based on one design—even though that design was never used. The original drawing was similar to, but not the same as, the model telephone that Bell introduced to the public.

1876: A PUBLIC DEMONSTRATION

Heat and high humidity settled over Philadelphia on June 25, 1876. The United States was celebrating the 100th **anniversary** of the Declaration of Independence. Philadelphia held a **Centennial Exposition.** Everything new and exciting was on display.

Elisha Gray submitted his telephone design for a patent on the same day as Alexander Graham Bell.

1876

Elisha Gray submits a caveat for his telephone invention.

Spencer Gore wins the first Wimbledon tennis championship in England.

Bell demonstrated a telephone such as the one shown here at the 1876 Centennial Exposition.

"THE DAY IS COMING WHEN TELEGRAPH WIRES WILL BE LAID ON TO HOUSES JUST LIKE WATER OR GAS—AND FRIENDS WILL CONVERSE WITH EACH OTHER WITHOUT LEAVING HOME."

ALEXANDER G. BELL IN A LETTER TO HIS FATHER, 1876

Twenty-nine-year-old Alexander Graham Bell signed up at the last minute to show his new invention. There was no more room in the exposition's "electrical" section. His booth was placed in the "education" section.

From the main building, Bell read a speech by William Shakespeare into the transmitter. Visitors gathered around the booth, 100 yards (30 m) away. Fascinated, they listened as Bell's words rang out over the receiver: "To be or not to be." Dom Pedro, the emperor of Brazil, was heard to have said, "My God, it talks!" The crowd buzzed with excitement. Everyone wanted to know more about Bell's telephone.

1876

Bell (right) demonstrates his telephone at Philadelphia's Centennial Exposition.

Heinz bottled ketchup is a new product at grocery stores.

PLENTY OF CHANGES

Newspaper headlines announced the miracle of Alexander Graham Bell's invention. Businesses rented the boxlike telephones for only $20 a year for two phones. In 1879, Alexander Graham Bell teamed up with the New England Telephone Company to create the National Bell Telephone Company, which sold telephones and service.

Telephone fever swept the country. A forest's worth of telephone poles sprang up on city blocks. Miles of phone wire formed a spider web against the sky.

In the beginning, every telephone call had to be connected by an operator. The telephone was a large wooden box, about the size of a shoebox. It had a fixed speaking cone and an earpiece on a wire. Most phone "numbers" were owners' names. To make a call, a person cranked a handle to alert the operator. The caller

| 1879 | Bell forms the National Bell Telephone Company. |

Thomas Edison (right) invents the lightbulb.

21

said, "Jane Jones, please." The operator connected the line.

The Lowell, Massachusetts, telephone service saw that this name situation could become a problem. There might be a dozen or more John Smiths or Mary Johnsons in a town. Lowell changed to phone numbers instead of names in 1879. The rest of the country soon followed.

1919: ROTARY TELEPHONES

By the turn of the century, 855,900 people owned telephones. Public coin phones provided service for callers in Hartford, Connecticut. Callers could place local and long-distance calls, although New York-to-California calls were not possible until 1915.

The number of calls made daily put a strain on the telephone system. Operators could handle only so many calls a day.

1919

The rotary telephone (left) is offered to the general public.

World War I officially ends on June 28 with the signing of the Treaty of Versailles.

By 1915, switchboard operators across the United States were busily connecting callers.

A better means of connecting phones needed to be found.

Attempts at making rotary, or dial, phones were tried in Milwaukee, Wisconsin, as early as 1896. A caller could now dial "Jane Jones at number 606" and be connected. Bell Telephone Company began offering rotary phones to the general public in 1919. But dial-it-yourself technology flopped. Rotary phones were not widely used until the mid-1950s.

Phone numbers changed dramatically. So many people had telephones that the phone company needed a better, more accurate way to direct calls. By the 1950s, phone numbers had two letters and five numbers. Jane Jones's number became PE8-2606. In 1958, the phone company began phasing out letters. All-number dialing began in

1958 | All-number dialing is introduced.

The National Aeronautics and Space Administration (NASA) is founded to head up the U.S. space program.

Wichita Falls, Texas. That is the system used today.

1962: ADDING SERVICE

In 1962, Bell Labs added **digital** technology to their telephone service. This change made telephone connections cheaper and more efficient. Digital technology paved the way for the services that phone users enjoy today. The digital network made 9-1-1 emergency calls possible—and saved thousands of lives.

A digital network provides call-waiting and caller ID. Now, people never miss an important call. And they can avoid conversations they'd rather not have.

More importantly, digital networking connected computers and communications in distant locations. Before digital

> ### TELSTAR I
>
> IN 1962, BELL LABORATORIES BUILT AND LAUNCHED *TELSTAR I*, THE FIRST ORBITING COMMUNICATIONS SATELLITE. THIS SATELLITE MADE QUICK WORLDWIDE CONNECTIONS. SOUND QUALITY IMPROVED ON LONG-DISTANCE CALLS. TODAY, THOUSANDS OF COMMUNICATIONS SATELLITES CIRCLE EARTH.

1962

Bell Laboratories launches *Telstar I,* a communications satellite.

Rachel Carson (right) publishes *Silent Spring* and launches the environmental movement in the United States.

Bell Labs develops digital telephone networking.

Musician Bob Dylan becomes famous singing "Blowin' in the Wind."

The princess phone added style, design, and color to telephones. One popular color was robin's egg blue.

networks, computers were stand-alone machines. They could not connect, or "talk," to computers in other towns and cities. Telephone technology links individual computers with the rest of the world.

By the 1960s, telephones had become a decorating statement. Small desk phones called princess phones became the rage. The boring all-black phones of the 1950s gave way to pale pink and baby blue. In 1963, touch-tone phones replaced dials, although some people still have dial phones.

In 1964, a deaf dentist asked a deaf scientist to figure out how to attach a telephone to a **Teletype** machine. Many years later, this technology invented by James Marsters and Robert Weitchrecht became the basis for today's online chat rooms.

1963
Phones offer touch-tone dialing.

President John F. Kennedy is assassinated in Dallas, Texas.

1964
James Marsters and Robert Weitchrecht develop voice-generated typing technology.

The Beatles' "She Loves You" becomes number one in record sales.

CHAPTER FIVE

THE TELEPHONE TODAY

Today's telephones ring, beep, and chime a melody. A phone fits in a pocket, and people can call from malls, movie theaters, or Mom's house. This is definitely *not* the telephone of Bell's day. Yes, phones still transmit and receive, but transistors, batteries, and microchips power today's phone service. To help callers make their connections, telephones come with speed dialing and a personal phone book.

Phones invade every aspect of modern life. People call while driving, eating, and grocery shopping. Phones sneak

People talk on telephones from malls, theaters, and supermarkets.

1985

There are 204,000 cell phone users in the United States.

The Discovery Channel begins broadcasting on cable television.

into bedrooms, bathrooms, and gym locker rooms. Today's family has several phones. It also has a couple of phone numbers and often a telephone-linked Internet access. What happened to Bell's big box on the wall?

2003: 1.3 BILLION CELL PHONES

As early as the 1940s, phone companies began making mobile phones. They became standard equipment in police and military vehicles. The first models were chunky, heavy, and not very convenient.

Today's cell phones are the great-grandchildren of early mobile telephones. When cell phones first hit the market, consumers couldn't buy them fast enough. In 1985, the United States had about 204,000 cell phone

2003

About 1.3 billion people worldwide use cell phones.

The United States and its allies invade Iraq (left).

users. That number jumped to 1,600,000 in three years. By 2003, nearly 140 million people in the United States had cell phones. Worldwide, cell phone users number 1.3 billion people.

Because of the telephone, people no longer need drums, flares, or signal flags. Quick communications, either by phone or Internet, have become expected. Few people can imagine living without a telephone for even a day. And all this began with a single message: "Mr. Watson, come here! I want you."

2004

An earthquake in Morocco kills more than 500 people.

There are more than a billion cell phones in use, including this one in Marrakech, Morocco.

anniversary (an-uh-VUR-suh-ree) An anniversary is the celebration of a specific date, such as a birthday or wedding. The United States celebrated the 100th anniversary of the Declaration of Independence in 1876.

apparatus (ap-uh-RAT-uhss) An apparatus is a machine or piece of equipment. In 1875, Bell produced a harp apparatus that sent sound using reeds.

caveat (CAH-vee-aht) A caveat is a paper filed with a patent office that presents a design for a new invention that has not yet been built. Gray filed a caveat for a patent on February 14, 1876.

Centennial Exposition (sen-TEN-ee-uhl ek-spoh-ZIH-shuhn) The Centennial Exposition is a fair that celebrates the 100th year of an event. In 1876, Bell demonstrated his telephone at Philadelphia's Centennial Exposition.

diaphragm (DYE-uh-fram) A diaphragm is a disc used to change sound into an electrical signal. Reis's transmitter had a metal contact against a paperlike diaphragm.

digital (DIJ-uh-tuhl) Digital describes a number system for recording text, images, or sound in a form that can be used on a computer. In 1962, Bell Labs added digital technology to its telephone service.

magnetostriction (mag-NET-oh-STRIKT-shuhn) Magnetostriction is a scientific theory that magnets can make metal stretch or shrink. Reis's receiver used the scientific theory of magnetostriction.

patent (PAT-uhnt) A patent is a piece of paper from the government that gives a person or company the exclusive rights to make or sell a new invention. James McDonough applied for a patent on April 10, 1876.

receiver (ri-SEE-vur) A receiver is a machine that collects pulses, sounds, signals, or beams from a transmitter. On March 10, 1876, Bell and Watson succeeded in sending a voice message from a transmitter to a receiver.

Teletype (TEL-uh-tipe) A Teletype is a machine that mechanically changes electrical signals into typed words. In 1964, a deaf dentist asked a deaf scientist to figure out how to attach a telephone to a Teletype machine.

transmitter (transs-MIT-uhr) A transmitter sends pulses, sounds, signals, or beams of some kind. Many scientists believe that Reis's transmitter was the first machine to send a human voice.

vibrations (vye-BRAY-shuhnz) Vibrations are the movement or shaking of an object, usually caused by sound or touch. A bone passes on the vibrations of sound.

FOR FURTHER INFORMATION

AT THE LIBRARY

Nonfiction

Gearhart, Sarah. *The Telephone*. New York: Atheneum, 1999.

* Haven, Kendall F. *Alexander Graham Bell: Inventor and Visionary*. Danbury, Conn.: Franklin Watts, 2003.

* McCormick, Anita Louise. *The Invention of the Telegraph and Telephone in American History*. Berkeley Heights, N.J.: Enslow Publishers, Inc., 2004.

Noyed, Robert B. *Alexander Graham Bell: Inventor*. Chanhassen, Minn.: The Child's World, 2003.

Tomecek, Steve. *What a Great Idea: Inventions That Changed the World*. New York: Scholastic, 2003.

Fiction

Stine, R. L. *Phone Calls: Phone Calls*. New York: Simon Pulse, 1990.

* Books marked with a star are challenge reading material for those reading above grade level.

ON THE WEB

Visit our home page for lots of links about the telephone: *http://www.childsworld.com/links.html*

Note to Parents, Teachers, and Librarians: We routinely check our Web links to make sure they're safe, active sites—so encourage your readers to check them out!

PLACES TO VISIT OR CONTACT

BellSouth Center
675 West Peachtree Street NE
Atlanta, GA 30375
404/529–0971

The Museum of Communications
7000 East Marginal Way South
Seattle, WA 98108
206/767–3012

The Telephone Historical Centre
10437 83rd Avenue
Edmonton, Alberta, Canada T6E 4T5
780/433-1010

INDEX

Bell, Alexander Graham, 11, 12, 13, 14–20
Bell, Eliza, 14–15
Bell Laboratories, 25
Bell, Mabel, 15
Bell, Melly, 15
Bell, Melville, 15
Bell Telephone Company, 13, 24
Butterworth, Benjamin, 13

call-waiting, 25
caller ID, 25
caveats, 18
cell phones, 28–29
Centennial Exposition, 19
colonial days, 7–8

computers, 26

diaphragm, 11
digital technology, 25–26
directories, 24
drum signals, 6, 7

electricity, 9–10
emergency calls, 25

Franklin, Ben, 8

Game Boy Advance, 28
Gray, Elisha, 11, 18–19
Gray, Stephen, 9

harp apparatus, 16–17
Hayes, Rutherford B., 22

Henry, Joseph, 9–10

Lovelace, Francis, 8

magnetostriction, 12
mail service, 7–8
McDonough, James W., 11, 12–13
Michigan State Telephone Company, 24
mobile phones, 28
Morse code, 10
Morse, Samuel F. B., 10
multifunction phones, 28
multiple telegraph, 15

National Bell Telephone Company, 21

operators, 21–22

patents, 12–13, 17, 18
Pedro, Dom, 20
phone numbers, 21–22, 24–25
princess phones, 26

Reis, Philipp, 11–12
Reis Receiver, 11–12
Reis Transmitter, 11
Richards, Laura Elizabeth, 12
rotary phones, 24

smoke signals, 6
soup can phones, 6

telegraph, 11, 15
teleloge, 12, 13
Telestar I satellite, 25
Teletype machines, 26
touch-tone phones, 26

vibrations, 14–15

Watson, Thomas, 16, 17–18

Yellow Pages, 24

ABOUT THE AUTHOR

BARBARA A. SOMERVILL IS THE AUTHOR OF MANY BOOKS FOR CHILDREN. SHE LOVES LEARNING AND SEES EVERY WRITING PROJECT AS A CHANCE TO LEARN NEW INFORMATION OR GAIN A NEW UNDERSTANDING. MS. SOMERVILL GREW UP IN NEW YORK STATE, BUT HAS ALSO LIVED IN TORONTO, CANADA; CANBERRA, AUSTRALIA; CALIFORNIA; AND SOUTH CAROLINA. SHE CURRENTLY LIVES WITH HER HUSBAND IN SIMPSONVILLE, SOUTH CAROLINA.